IMAGES
of America

AROUND CLYMER

Born and raised in the Philadelphia area, George Clymer (1739–1813) was a businessman and member of the Continental Congress. He also became one of only six individuals to sign both the Declaration of Independence in 1776 and the US Constitution ratified in 1789.

ON THE COVER: Standing in front of the Stanton Building on West Main Street in 1916 is a theatrical group, perhaps rehearsing a play that would be performed in the upstairs theater.

IMAGES
of America

AROUND CLYMER

Rod Beckerink

ARCADIA
PUBLISHING

Published by Arcadia Publishing
Charleston, South Carolina

Printed in the United States of America

Library of Congress Control Number: 2024934660

For all general information, please contact Arcadia Publishing:
Telephone 843-853-2070
Fax 843-853-0044
E-mail sales@arcadiapublishing.com

Visit us on the Internet at www.arcadiapublishing.com

For all the residents of Clymer, past, present, and future.

"For an American who had the great and priceless privilege of being raised in a small town there always remains with him nostalgic memories."

—Dwight D. Eisenhower

CONTENTS

ACKNOWLEDGMENTS

This photographic glimpse of the history of Clymer is the result of a collaborative effort made by the contributions of many individuals. First and foremost, the volunteers of the Clymer Area Historical Society greatly aided the gathering and organizing of material. Cindy Willink and Suzanne Rhebergen, as town historians, present and past, helped fact-check the photographs and accompanying stories. Along with them are the "Tuesday morning crew" of Janet Heslink, Sheila Hawkins, Vicki Smith, Susan Rice, Marlea Brown, and Nancy VanderSchaaff who work tirelessly to preserve, protect, and share the history of Clymer. I would also thank the many individuals, including LouJean White and Jim Thompson, who shared their personal stories, memories, and photographs. Lastly, the late Marguerite VanderSchaaff, town historian in the 1960s and 1970s, devotedly kept scrapbooks and binders of newspaper articles and local events, without which would leave us today at a loss for much that took place in Clymer from the early 1900s until the late 1970s. Her foresighted efforts to record and preserve Clymer's 20th-century history provide a valuable written record that supplements much of the photographic record of Clymer. Unless otherwise noted, photographs appear courtesy of the Clymer Area Historical Society.

INTRODUCTION

Tucked into the far southwest corner of the southern tier of New York state is the small rural community of Clymer. Perhaps it is not that different from hundreds of other villages and towns across the country in the sense that it was established by its founding fathers, grew with the arrival of more settlers, and eventually a community established itself with homes and businesses. What becomes very clear in small rural towns is the degree to which most people are interconnected with each other. Locals conduct business with each other, their children go to school together, they attend weddings and funerals, go to church, and acknowledge each other with a friendly wave of the hand while passing on the street. When those factors are coupled with a population in which many share a common cultural heritage, an even stronger bond is created among the citizens. If you grew up and spent most of your life there, you probably heard numerous stories, some true, others perhaps embellished, of memorable events and accomplishments of this sports team or that individual, and how life seemed much simpler, maybe even better, in the reminiscent eye of the storyteller. If you were raised in Clymer and moved away at some later time, there is little doubt that the town left a lasting impression on some part of the person you became later in life. As a friend often remarks, "You can take the boy out of the country, but you can't take the country out of the boy." What this modest effort hopes to accomplish with the images found on the following pages is to provide a brief glimpse into Clymer's past as a way of explaining the Clymer of today. It is a town built on proud traditions, whose people display an independent and entrepreneurial spirit, and of families with deep ancestral roots whose businesses, farms, churches, and schools continue to shape the community of today.

Established in the virgin woodland forests of western New York in the 1820s, Clymer went through early growing pains to establish itself, including the survival of a financial crisis in the 1830s, which sent some initial settlers farther west. When the Holland Land Company began recruiting Dutch immigrants to settle in Clymer in the late 1830s and early 1840s, their arrival in the years that followed breathed new life into Clymer, and by the Civil War in the 1860s, the town bustled with businesses like tanneries and gristmills. With the arrival of the railroad in 1869, commerce continued to expand with transportation connections to markets along the more populated eastern seaboard. For the rest of the 1800s, Clymer continued to flourish as more Dutch immigrants arrived, cleared more land, and pursued a better life for themselves and their families. By the early 1900s, Clymer had emerged as a thriving community based on agriculture and related businesses. The inextricable commercial connection between the farmer and the local businessman revealed their dependence on each other. Without the businessman, the farmer was not helped financially by getting their crops, milk, and livestock to market. Without the farmer, the businessman did not have customers to sell machinery, grain, and lumber. Over the years, some businesses came and went while others changed names, expanded, and evolved. The same was true for the small family farm. With new production techniques and modern machinery, the size of the family farm grew throughout the 1900s.

That mutually beneficial economic relationship, along with the reality of the rural location of Clymer, contributed in other ways to the development of the community. With an entrepreneurial and independent spirit, the people of Clymer would not wait for the conveniences of the world to reach them. Instead, they created their own volunteer fire department and established a locally owned and capitalized bank, an electric company, a telephone company, and a water company, all with local boards of directors and trustees. In addition, as the country looked at educational reform as the wave of the future, Clymer was the first township in Chautauqua County to centralize its school system and, over a matter of just a few years, close its one-room schoolhouses as all students were brought together under one roof. Today, while most of those utilities have merged into larger corporations, new business ventures appear throughout the town, especially with the arrival in the late 1970s of the Amish to the Clymer community.

Many of the photographs that appear in this book are from the early and mid-1900s. It was during this time that Clymer, not unlike the rest of the country, experienced tremendous technological changes in transportation and communication. The horse and buggy gave way to the automobile, writing postcards gave way to making a phone call, and life in a small town changed in many ways. That transformation can be seen in many of the photographs throughout this book. Where life in the early 1900s was dominated by hard work, determination, and the horse, by the 1950s, that way of life certainly had changed—at least where the horse was concerned. When the Great Depression hit and was shortly followed by World War II, the future seemed uncertain. Following World War II, though, Clymer emerged, as did the rest of the country, with new energy. In Clymer's case, farms and businesses reached new levels of success, the school continued to expand with the population of the country, and the town came up with a novel way to celebrate their Dutch heritage with the creation of a tulip festival.

Today, the town still retains some of its Dutch character and tradition. The windmills continue to welcome visitors coming into town, tulips remain a popular springtime flower, and some of those family-run stores like Neckers Company and the Dutch Village Restaurant still open their doors to welcome customers. Yet it is a town going through a new transformation. As young people leave the area to pursue careers elsewhere, the Amish have settled in Clymer in search of the same opportunities as the Dutch immigrants did in the 1800s. New Amish homes and Amish-owned businesses, some with solar panels, and small one-room Amish schools can be found scattered throughout the township, making it seem like, as baseball player Yogi Berra put it, "déjà vu all over again" for the ongoing evolution of Clymer into the 21st century.

One

EARLY LIFE

FOUNDING SETTLERS
AND DUTCH IMMIGRANTS

Created in early 1821 by an act of the New York State Legislature, the town of Clymer initially also included the modern-day townships of French Creek, Mina, and Sherman. Within 10 years, those three towns had struck off on their own, and the remaining 36 square mile Clymer township began to take on its own identity, evolving over the years into what it is today. Exactly how the town was named is not clear. Traditional lore is that at the first town meeting in April 1821, council members debated over which founding father to choose as the town's namesake, finally arriving at George Clymer, signer of both the Declaration of Independence and the US Constitution. Yet this story overlooks the fact the town was already identified as Clymer when the New York State Legislature acted to create Clymer in February 1821. Although there is no written evidence, the name might be the result of the work of Joseph Ellicott and Paul Busti, two Philadelphia land agents of the Holland Land Company hired to survey and sell land in the wilderness of western New York state, including Chautauqua County. Ellicott and Busti, as well as Clymer, were all from the Philadelphia area. Yet any definitive connection that might today shed light on the naming origin went up in flames in 1911 when a fire in Albany destroyed nearly all early New York colonial and state legislative records.

As Clymer emerged from the wooded wilderness and land was cleared in the 1820s and 1830s, names appear in the property records that might seem unfamiliar today, unless you took a stroll through the Eastside Cemetery or glanced at street names. Some of these names were Rice, Cleveland, Greeley, Card, Freeman, Knowlton, and Brownell. In the 1830s, a nationwide financial crisis led some early settlers to abandon their land and head farther west to cheaper land. This event, along with economic and political despair in Europe, led to a wave of immigrants from the Netherlands searching for new land and opportunity. By the mid-1840s, the first Dutch settlers arrived in Clymer with dozens more families following them in the years to come. By the turn of the century, the town was predominantly Dutch, and that shaped Clymer's personality and progress for much of the 1900s.

Although Horace Greeley only lived in Clymer for a short period of time and visited occasionally, those visits to his parents, who moved to the Clymer area from Vermont in the 1820s, perhaps shaped his popular suggestion, "Go West, young man, and grow up with the country." After a couple of months living with his parents in the summer of 1831, Greeley left for the newspaper publishing world, eventually becoming editor of the influential *New York Tribune*. Greeley was the liberal Republican-Democrat presidential candidate in 1872, losing to incumbent president U.S. Grant. (Courtesy of the National Portrait Gallery.)

Records show that tanneries were established in Clymer as early as the 1830s, and as many as three operated in the area in the later 1800s. Shown here in 1885 is one of the larger ones, Rice, Emery & Company, which employed upwards of 30 men and was eventually sold to the United States Leather Company. The tanning process used ashes from farmers clearing land and burning trees, giving farmers an additional source of income. In the latter half of the 1900s, Meyerink Milling Company was located on the site of this tannery. Among the work crew, notice the worker wearing wooden shoes seated in the front row.

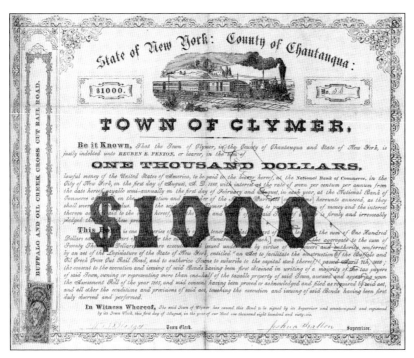

The first railroad reached Clymer in 1866 as part of an effort to link the new oil industry of northwest Pennsylvania to Lake Erie. The Buffalo & Oil Creek Cross Cut Railroad was partially funded through the sale of bonds like the one depicted in this image.

A general store has existed on the northwest corner of the center of Clymer for over 125 years. Easily recognized and known for the last 110 years as Neckers Company, this photograph from the late 1800s shows a gathering of townsfolk in front of the store then owned by A.G. Beach.

Taking advantage of the abundant forests in the area, sawmills have always been an important element of Clymer's local economy. An early example of this is Henry Deuink's sawmill from the late 1800s, where logs were cut for the lumber used to build barns and houses in the area. Shown here are, from left to right, Henry Deuink, Clarence Legters, James Cordia, Henry Wassink, and David Bensink.

Built by Herman Haverkamp in the 1880s, this home was one of the earliest brick structures in Clymer. With double brick walls, the house has withstood the elements over the years, and today, it serves as part of the museum of the Clymer Area Historical Society. The Haverkamp Huis, along with its barn, houses a growing collection of artifacts, memorabilia, and records of Clymer's history.

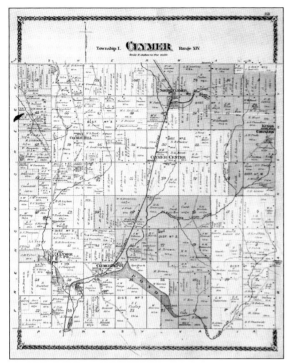

These two maps from 1881 show the growth of Clymer, which includes smaller hamlets such as Clymer Depot, Clymer Center, Clymer Hill, and North Clymer. It is safe to conclude that some of this growth was due to the completion of the railroad in 1869, connecting Clymer to areas north toward Lake Erie and Buffalo as well as Corry, Pennsylvania, and beyond to the south. What also becomes clear from examining this map more closely are the Dutch surnames listed as property owners. As these families grew generationally in the late 1800s and early 1900s, Clymer's Dutch character became quite clear, first in the Clymer Hill area and eventually throughout the township.

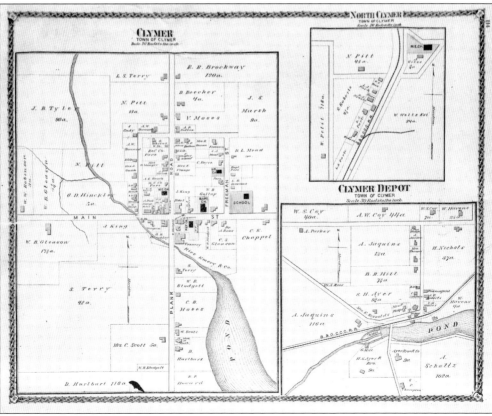

14

As time passed into the 20th century and families became more established in the community, reunions provided a chance for members to gather and reconnect with those who had moved away. Usually occurring in the summer, reunions provided an opportunity for people to gather at a home for a picnic and games. Gathered here in 1935 is the Esselink reunion on the front porch of a home on Cabbage Hill Road.

Looking westward down the hill on current Route 474 toward North Clymer, the United Brethren Church is located on the left, just above the Wiggers farm. The building was moved down through the fields and across from the railroad tracks in North Clymer to establish the Evangelical United Brethren Church, eventually being torn down in the late 1900s.

Situated halfway between Clymer and Panama as well as being located along the railroad between Clymer and Sherman, North Clymer had its own post office, feed mill, and a handful of small stores and shops. Looking in a southeasterly direction from Raspas Hill, the current feed mill can be seen in the top right center.

Clymer contributed greatly when the United States found itself involved in conflict. The Civil War drew large numbers of immigrants into service as soldiers, sometimes taking the draft spots of those who could afford to pay someone to take their place. In this photograph is Pvt. John TeWinkle, who served in the 1st New York Infantry. He survived the war and settled on Clymer Hill. Over 100 men from the Clymer area served during the Civil War, and 27 did not return alive.

Rural free delivery mail service came to Clymer on September 15, 1902, and that meant citizens did not have to go into town to pick up their mail. The mailmen and their numbered route wagons in front of Kooman's hardware store are ready to head out on their daily rounds. The only one identified is Otis Fardink, second from right.

While there is one grocery store in Clymer today, in the first half of the 1900s there were several stores from which to choose. Shown here in a photograph from the 1920s is the Flickinger Store, located in the current post office. The Independent Order of Odd Fellows met on the upper floor and actually built the structure, renting out the space on the first floor.

Built in 1908 by Sam Ton, Clymer's town hall provided a gathering place for community events, including official business and recreation. A basketball court on the second floor served both the high school and the Flying Dutchmen teams in the 1920s and 1930s. A vestibule on the first floor provided warmth and shelter for the occasional vagrant passing through town. Eventually, the building was dismantled in the late 1960s.

In a late-1800s view from the southwest looking into town, one can see the steeple of the Methodist church and the bridge on the western end of Main Street. The split rail fence in the foreground is approximately where today's hardware store is located, while the bridge and stream were much closer to town than they are today.

Because of its impact on farmers, one of the most important factories in town was the milk condensery. Located off Mill Street (now Knowlton Road) and right next to the railroad tracks, the milk plant took daily deliveries of raw milk from farmers who brought their milk cans drawn by horse and wagon, condensed the milk into a powder form through a heating and evaporation process, and shipped the finished product off to the markets by rail. The house on the left was moved across the fields to East Main Street, where it is the home of Irving Legters.

The milling of grain was an essential requirement in a farming community, and Meyerink Milling Company located right in town provided such a service. Photographed here is a farmer who is likely loading burlap bags of ground corn or other grains to be used as supplemental feed for the dairy herd.

Clymer's first machine shop was part of the G.H. Tenpas enterprise and was located in this building at the back of the Tenpas property. Such a shop gave locals a place to get machinery repaired as well as having specific equipment fabricated. Seen here in 1911 are, from left to right, employees unidentified, Ray Renskers, and unidentified.

Electricity was first produced in Clymer in 1913 using this coal-fired steam generator located at the rear of the Tenpas property. Seen in the photograph are Garret Tenpas's father-in-law, Henry Bennink, and his dog Shep. Tenpas produced electricity both here and at Jaquin's Pond by hydropower until Niagara Mohawk bought out Tenpas in the 1930s.

It might not be recognizable as today's Spitzer Funeral Home and Windmill Flower and Gifts next door, but this photograph is what a pedestrian saw in the late 1800s. Owned by O.J. Damon initially, William Kearns took over in 1915 only to sell to Clarence Spitzer in 1919. Spitzer and his son stayed in the funeral home business into the late 1900s but sold the furniture store to Kenneth Kooman in 1947, who then sold it to Andrew Hutton in 1964.

This 1915 street view looking westward from approximately in front of the current bank shows the dirt roads along with the horse and buggies lined up in front of Neckers Brothers on the south side of Main Street and Neckers Company past the intersection on the north side. It is notable just how many trees grew in the middle of town at that time, especially around the Hinckley house.

This 1922 aerial view from the southeast of Clymer shows the Wassink dam and pond in the foreground and the town on the horizon at the far end of the pond. Throughout the 20th century, the pond remained a focal point of the community, receiving financial aid for dredging in the 1970s and serving today as a backdrop for the town park and pavilion located on the west side of the pond.

Built in the late 1870s, the White schoolhouse, sometimes referred to as "the Union school," was a wooden frame structure that stood in a grove of trees roughly where today's school is located. It served all grade levels of students from town until 1913, when the first brick school was built. The White schoolhouse was moved across the street and stood until the winter of 2002, collapsing from the weight of heavy snow.

The Eagle Hotel located at the center of Clymer provided visitors with overnight accommodation while on their journey. The horse-drawn omnibus seen in this photograph provided transportation to the train depot, including to dignitaries during the 1872 rally to reelect President Grant.

The Eagle Hotel also hosted a variety of gatherings like the 4th of July Dance and the New Year's Ball, as indicated by the tickets shown here from 1864 and 1876.

NEW YEAR'S BALL.

The Company of YOURSELF and LADY is respectfully invited to attend a BALL to be held at the

Eagle House, in Clymer,

ON FRIDAY EVENING, JANUARY 1st 1864.

MUSIC:—MASON'S BAND.

LUTHER MASON, Floor Manager.

A. H. BAKER, - - - - - - PROPRIETOR.

The southeast corner of town has changed greatly in the past 100 years. The three buildings at the center of the photograph no longer exist, while the Newhouse wagon shop at the far left is today's Dutch Village Restaurant, which itself expanded toward the intersection in the late 1990s as the other structures were demolished.

Constructed in 1915, the Stanton Building initially housed the post office and telephone company on the first floor and a small theatrical hall on the second floor. Following a bad fire in the early 1920s, it was rebuilt with a portico as seen here in 1922. In later years, the portico was removed when it housed the Damcott-Jones American Legion and, beginning in 1962, the town library.

Before the automobile was common, church attendance in the winter needed shelter for the horses during Sunday services. Shown here are the large horse barns located at the rear of the Abbe Reformed Church property. The last major addition was completed in 1919 and not torn down until the early 1950s.

Without refrigeration on the farm, farmers needed to make a daily trip to the milk plant with their milk can-laden, horse-drawn wagons with the previous evening and morning's milk. Photographed here in 1915 is Henry Wassink with his daughter Eunice in the process of delivering the milk cans to the plant on Mill Street. Each of these milk cans held 10 gallons of milk, making this quite a substantial load.

Caflisch Lumber Company, at one time located on Jaquin's Pond, moved major operations somewhat closer to Clymer at a site above the old dam at Jaquin's. This aerial photograph from the 1940s shows the mill operation and lumberyard with Clymer about half a mile to the west. Today, Heil Transportation occupies this property.

Before the series of financial crises of the 1830s, which initiated banking regulation and the printing of paper currency, banks often printed their own money. An example is shown in this image of a bill issued by Atlas Bank in 1847, its only year of existence. (Courtesy of Bryan Caflisch.)

Chris Christensen arrived in Clymer from Denmark in 1914. After several jobs, he started a livery business in 1918, often driving traveling salesmen from the train depot to businesses throughout the community. The business operated out of today's credit union and insurance building. Eventually, Christensen became an automobile dealer operating out of the Eagle Hotel. (Courtesy of Julie Ganske.)

Jaquin's, sometimes referred to as Clymer Depot, was a very busy location in the early 1900s. Situated right beside the railroad tracks, it was the first location of the train depot until it was moved to Mill Street (now Knowlton Road) about one mile to the south. Also located here was an early sawmill, seen at the extreme left of this 1920s photograph, and a dam built by Garret Tenpas to provide hydroelectric power to customers. Just a few years later, a large sawmill and lumberyard operated by the Caflisch family began operations on the pond created by the Tenpas dam, creating water rights usage litigation in the late 1920s. (Courtesy of Dan Caflisch.)

Originally constructed as the Baptist church in 1868 and purchased by Garret Tenpas in 1910, what eventually became known as the Tenpas building, at one time or another, housed apartments on the second floor, a town water supply tank in place of the steeple, and a jewelry store, bank, and post office on the first floor. The Tenpas enterprise also included a streetside gas station and a diner on the west side. The building would be dismantled in 1968–1969 to make way for a new bank.

What stands today as the original part of the Dutch Village Restaurant began as the J.W. Newhouse wagon and harness shop in the early 1900s, seen above in 1910. The photograph below shows the interior of the Newhouse shop; clearly seen around the shop are wares such as harnesses, horse collars, and something new to the streets around town: bicycles. Seen in both photographs is J.W. "Bill" Newhouse, and in the above photograph, he is with his son Alfred.

The horse-drawn omnibus, driven here by George Legters in 1910, conveyed merchants and travelers to and from Clymer to the train depot located just to the east of town at Jaquin's. In the background, one can see a house and the White school. When a new brick school was built in 1912–1913, the house was split into two and moved down Mohawk Street to create two homes while the school was moved directly across Main Street.

Like the omnibus, the horse-drawn sleigh, driven here in 1917 by Merle Raspas, transported people during the winter months over the snowy roads to their destination. Raspas was one of four soldiers from the Clymer area to die during service to their country during World War I. The small structure next to the Eagle Hotel, at various times, was a restaurant, shoe repair shop, barbershop, and lastly, the town library until the early 1960s, when the books were moved down the street to the Stanton Building.

By the early 1900s, technology was rapidly changing how work was done on the farm. Even though much of the work was still labor-intensive, much more work could be done and, as a result, family farms increased in size, in terms of both acreage and livestock. The steam engine used here powered a thresher while 11 workers were doing various jobs around the barn during the harvest process.

When Sam Ton (left) and Garrett Habink (right) purchased this property from Aaron Parker in 1912, they established the Clymer Lumber Company. Seen here in 1922, the company was located immediately east of the cemetery on East Main Street and provided all the construction materials necessary to finish the building project. The company remained in business until the 1960s when the property was taken over by Gallup and TenHaken.

These two photographs taken from the water tower vantage point atop the Tenpas building provide elevated views of Clymer from the early 1920s. The photograph above shows the view of the center of town looking westward toward Cutting. Notable is the alleyway at the back of Neckers Company connecting North Center Street to Maple Avenue to the west as well as the pitched roof on the Stanton Building on West Main Street. The photograph below shows the view of homes and backyard gardens looking northward out of town. Barely visible in the trees is the tower of Abbe Reformed Church.

Many homes around Clymer were wood frame construction built in the late 1800s and early 1900s. Fairly typical styles were these two homes that still stand on the west side of North Center Street at the edge of town.

The importance of the railroad is on display in this 1913 photograph of a shipment of new Ford automobiles on flatbed railcars. Having arrived by train in North Clymer, the Model Ts were then unloaded at the railroad siding across from the grain mill seen in the background. The final destination of the automobiles is unknown, but their presence was certainly a sign of the times as modes of transportation changed in the early 1900s.

Businesses in Clymer abounded in the early 1900s. The image above was taken in front of the Neckers Brothers store, with Albert Neckers Jr. at the reins. In the photograph below, with Walter Kooman, the usefulness of the peddler's wagon becomes evident. It was used to sell and deliver goods to customers around the Clymer area to increase sales by going out on the rural roads to make sales to farm families. As a result, those customers did not have to make as many trips into town. First owned by the Kooman store and then by Neckers Brothers, the wagon is part of the collection of the Clymer Area Historical Society today.

Sitting on the northwest corner of town today is Neckers Company. Before the 1990s, there were four businesses operating at one time or another, including Legters Brothers meat market. Also included was a hardware store under different proprietors. At the time of this photograph in 1910, it was Kooman Brothers. Seen here are, from left to right, Cliff Kooman, Guy Johnson, John Kooman, Fred Kooman, and unidentified.

A 1943 fender bender involving a coal truck and a feed truck at the main intersection in front of Neckers Company and the Texaco gas station prompted calls for a flashing light to control traffic. In time, that light was installed, first stopping traffic on Center Street and recently becoming a four-way red light for all traffic.

The development of business and commerce in Clymer was closely tied to the presence of the railroad. As a result, and out of convenience to all people, the train depot originally located at Jaquin's was moved closer to town and adjacent to the milk plant, as seen in these two photographs. Commercial shipments were received and sent from this location as was passenger train service for destinations north and south of Clymer. Passenger service was discontinued in the late 1940s, and all rail service ended by the early 1980s. Shortly thereafter, the rails were taken out, and today, an effort is being made to include the abandoned railbed in the growing Rails-to-Trails network.

Two

Everyday Life
Businesses and Farms

The close relationship between the farming and business communities is apparent when one begins to understand how reliant they were on each other. Without businesses like Meyerink Milling Company, Gallup and TenHaken, and Legters Brothers, the farmers would have found it difficult to prosper and be able to plant and harvest crops as well as get those same crops and livestock to market. Likewise, without the farmers, the businesses would not have had the customers to sell and repair machinery, mill grain, and provide lumber to build barns and houses. In addition to the businesses that had a direct working relationship with the farmers, several ancillary businesses like barbershops, restaurants, and hardware stores provided important services to everyone in the community. Over the years, some businesses came into existence and then disappeared, while others changed names, expanded, and evolved with the times. The same was true of the family farm. What started out as a small immigrant family operation in the 1800s expanded in the 1900s with the arrival of electricity, the combustion engine, and endless new technologies. The age of the horse gave way to the combustion engine and tractor. Milking cows by hand, filling milk cans, and carting them to the milk plant gave way to automatic milking machines, refrigerated bulk milk tanks, and daily visits by the milk truck to haul milk to the plant. By the mid-1900s, numerous dairy farms and their feed silos were a familiar sight dotting the countryside around Clymer. From the late winter maple sugaring season to springtime planting and from summertime baling of hay to the fall harvesting of corn and other crops, there was plenty of work to be done for farm families, especially for teenage sons. Yet for a variety of reasons, many of those family farms slowly disappeared in the latter half of the 20th century. Continually, more expensive automation made the family farm a difficult financial proposition. For many, the choice was going big or closing the barn doors. There were a few farms that went big, but dozens of small farms fell out of production. Yet again, with the arrival of a new group of people—in Clymer's case, the Amish—the town continues to experience an evolution in entrepreneurial business and farming.

In a photograph taken in front of Neckers Brothers, William Fardink sorts through crates and baskets of apples. Of special interest is the crate behind him stenciled as the National Biscuit Company, the forerunner of today's international Nabisco company.

The barbershop traditionally served as a social gathering place for men to share the news and stories of the day. Sometimes, a pool hall helped pass the time when no one needed a haircut. In this 1914 photograph, from left to right, Dr. ? Keyes, Bill TeWinkle, George Durand, Mike Cline, and proprietor Otis Fardink share a moment in the billiard room. In later years, Art Stoddard operated this barbershop, and just across the alleyway, one could find Jack Fair's barbershop.

Seen here in 1975, the North Clymer Agway has met the needs of area farmers searching for ways to improve their dairy's milk production. In existence for over 100 years, the grain mill has had quite a few owners as well as belonging to an evolution of different agricultural cooperatives. At one time, it also served as the post office for North Clymer.

The Hemink Grocery store and gas station were located at the triangle in North Clymer where Route 76 from Sherman meets Route 474 coming from Panama to the east and Clymer to the west. Built by Luke Hemink and his father, Bill, in 1937, it operated until the early 1980s, including a brief time as the North Clymer Post Office.

One of the most prominent homes in Clymer sat on the southwest corner of the village center. Built in the later 1800s by Otis D. Hinckley, who was a justice of the peace and a civil engineer and served on the Chautauqua County Board of Supervisors, the structure featured stately porch columns and iron fences around the yard. Stories were told of wonderful parties and parlor games held there in the late 1800s and early 1900s. Unfortunately, its demise came during the Great Depression when financial struggles and neglect led to the home being demolished and, shortly thereafter, replaced by a gas station. Today, a veterinarian's clinic and greenspace occupy this corner.

Very little is known of the company whose stock certificate is shown here. The North Clymer Oil and Gas Company existed in the early 1900s during the speculative heyday of the oil boom that began in northwestern Pennsylvania in the late 1800s. Its demise likely came as larger oil companies like Standard Oil expanded their control of the petroleum industry.

Five miles away and along the railroad tracks to northern Chautauqua County, the hamlet of North Clymer had its own general store, photographed here in 1913. Once owned by Henry Raspas and owned by Perry Hillberg at the time of the photograph, it was later known as Fardink's General Store. It was finally torn down in the 1950s as New York improved the safety of the Raspas Hill Road railroad crossing located across from the present-day feed mill.

Created in the 1930s and located on Mill Street at the southern end of the Clymer Pond, the Clymer Bag Company met a unique need of grain mills and farmers. Under the initial ownership of Marvin Holthouse, the company manufactured and repaired burlap bags used by grain mills to deliver mixes of oats, corn, and other grains to local dairy farmers to increase their milk production. The above photograph from the late 1940s shows owners and employees along with a display of some of the bags produced for area grain mills. Below, Jennie Cady (left) and Gertrude Bennink (right) are at their sewing machines repairing burlap bags.

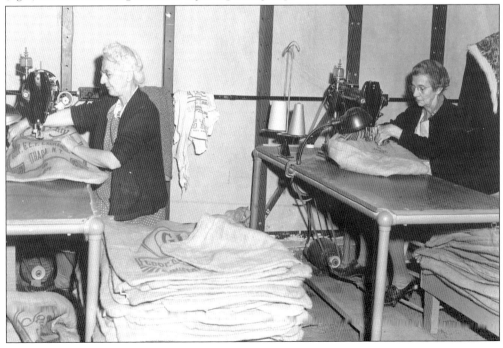

The Clymer Telephone Company began in 1915 as a private locally owned company meeting the needs of the people. The office location in the village changed over the years, as did its service, moving from switchboard operators and party lines to private lines and efficient long-distance calling. Seen in this photograph are operators Bea Reed (left) and Lenore Camper (right) handling switchboard duties in the 1950s.

The current post office building in Clymer was once a grocery store. From the early 1900s, Flickinger's operated until the 1930s when Earl and Ruth Beckerink began operating the Red and White grocery store until the late 1950s, giving the village three groceries in the mid-1900s. Also located on the building's second floor was the meeting hall for the Independent Order of Odd Fellows and its sister organization, the Rebekahs.

With its not-so-distant past connection to its roots in the Netherlands, Clymer maintained those ties to Holland during World War II. From late 1944 through 1945, the Dutch people experienced a "Hunger Winter" in which thousands starved to death. Pictured here in front of the Tenpas building and a large plaque with the names of soldiers serving in World War II from the Clymer area are, from left to right, Leonard Hogenboom, Garret Tenpas, Harold Legters, and Fred Vander Schaaff with a truck from Meyerink Milling Company loaded with crates of relief supplies destined for the home country.

For much of the 1900s, Clymer had a print shop and published newspapers. Versions included the *Clymer Dispatch*, the *Clymer Booster*, and lastly, the *Clymer Independent*. The last edition came off the press in 1969 when the publisher and printer Wayne Morrison moved to Ovid, New York, in the Finger Lakes region. On the walls in this photograph can be seen posters advertising a charity American Field Service basketball game at the high school and a ban on Sunday hunting in Clymer.

The Abbe Reformed Church and parsonage have been at their current location for almost 150 years, although both have been rebuilt once and remodeled numerous times. Shortly after Rev. Abraham Klerk arrived in 1913, he declared he could not live in the house, which prompted the church consistory to authorize a new parsonage. The old structure was split, moved up the street to become two new homes, and the new parsonage was constructed. Upon its completion in 1917, Reverend Klerk left Clymer. In this photograph, the parsonage is almost complete, and its builder, Sam Ton, is at the corner of the porch wearing an apron and hat.

From its creation in 1916, Legters Brothers meat market was the place to pick up all the ham and turkey needed for Thanksgiving and Christmas dinners as well as a wide variety of meats for any other occasion. Legters Brothers also served as cattle haulers for local farmers sending their livestock to market. Pictured here in 1941 are, from left to right, Clifford "Uncle Packy" Legters and brothers Harold, Howard "Cutch," and Everett Legters.

Another example of the way businesses changed locations and buildings served different purposes is seen in this photograph from 1909. Sitting on the southeast corner of the center of town and no longer just a hardware store, this building is also the post office, and the mail carriers are ready to head out to make their deliveries. In the photograph are, from left to right, Milton Rundell, Len Kooman, Otis Fardink, Arnold Wiggers, Guy Bennink, Tom Kniphuisen, and Will Kniphuisen.

A gas and service station has existed on the corner of Freeman and East Main Streets for almost 90 years. Originally located in front of the school and at the end of Mohawk Street, the building was moved to the current site in 1935 by owner Edgar TeCulver. Bought by Gail "Tommy" Thompson in 1952 and then sold to Troy Chase in 1967, Jim Thompson bought the station in 1971 at the time of this photograph.

A scene repeated across the town on the numerous farms, season after season, is a family participating in the grain harvest. With three hardworking draft horses at the lead and big brother Herbert at the reins, the Simmelink family works in the wheat field. From left to right, Irvin, Merrill, mother Mary holding Christina, Ruby, Ruth, and father Henry help where needed. While some members of the family remained in Clymer, others headed west to settle in eastern Washington state, where they established farms that are still in operation today, and the Simmelink name is emblazoned on the Washington State University tennis courts.

Until the modern tractor reached every farmer, horses continued to perform a considerable amount of heavy-duty work pulling farm equipment through the fields into the early 1950s. In this photograph from 1944, Henry Wassink walks his horses south of town on South Center Street with Meyerink Milling Company in the background.

Still in operation today, the North Clymer feed mill provided farmers in the northern part of the township with easy access to milling services. Located right next to the railroad tracks, the mill could easily ship and receive goods and grain and for some time even served as the post office. Pictured here in the 1920s are owners Wilton Wevers (left) and brother-in-law Clarence Legters (right).

Early in the morning and late in the afternoon, farmers like Glen Beckerink headed to the barn to milk the cows. Of all the work done on the farm, this task was the money maker for the dairy farmer. In this photograph from the 1950s, technology has eliminated milking cows by hand and replaced it with automated milking machines. Refrigerated bulk milk tanks with pickups by milk trucks also eliminated the farmer's trip to the milk plant in Clymer.

For farmers, the busiest times of the year were planting in the spring and harvesting in the summer and fall. Without machinery, this work would have been done all by hand and with original horsepower. Machinery allowed the farmer to increase the size of the farm, grow more crops, and milk more cows. Photographed above and below are grain threshers. Above is Garret Tenpas at the controls of the steam engine, which is connected to the thresher by a long drive belt. Thresher workers fed the thresher with harvested grain, which resulted in separating the grain from the chaff. Below is a photograph of just the thresher at a barn door opening.

The commerce taking place around the Tenpas building in 1952 created a busy street scene for anyone driving through town. Whether it was stopping for a fill-up at the gas station, a bite to eat at the diner, getting some cash at the bank, or mailing a letter at the post office, it was akin to today's one-stop store long before its time.

Before Lictus Keystone existed, Harris Kolstee operated the Keystone franchise in Clymer. Shown here in 1947, Kolstee stands with his fuel delivery truck at his farm on Mill Street (now Knowlton Road) at the southern end of the town pond.

Thompson Farms, which operated from the 1920s to the 1970s, included a Holstein dairy and poultry sales in a two-state area that went as far east as supplying resorts in the Catskills. Probably most well-known, though, was its potato operation, which marketed "Dutch Girl" potatoes in the grocery store and provided seed potatoes throughout the United States, including a shipment to Ecuador, South America, following a blight. The early 1950s photograph above shows, from left to right, Jim Thompson, Bill Ruff, and Ralph Thompson with a truckload of sacks of potatoes at the Clymer railroad depot. Below is a field of potatoes recently dug up and being bagged. (Both, courtesy of Jim Thompson.)

As progress brought tractors and more modern machinery to the farm, much work still required a great deal of manual labor. As farms increased in size, a true sense of community spirit and neighborliness was witnessed when farmers pooled their varied machinery and labor together, especially at harvest time, as seen here and repeated all over town. In the photograph above from 1937, workers gather on the Wassink farm with a tractor and thresher. Below are farmers in 1947 taking a coffee break on the Wassink farm. When work was completed at one farm, men and machinery moved on to the next farm until all the crops were harvested.

Late winter and early spring brought on the maple sugar season. Farmers would prepare all year, building up firewood piles for the sugarhouse. As daytime temperatures rose with cold, freezing nights, the sap started to flow, nourishing trees for springtime. Trees were tapped, buckets hung, and sap gathered and taken to the sugarhouse where the boiling process reduced sap to syrup. In these two photographs, sap is being gathered the traditional way. Above is Red Crandall with a team of horses and sledge in the snowy sugarbush on the Bert Lictus farm south of town. Below, in 1942, Henry Wassink gathers sap by horse and wagon in his sugarbush on Mill Street.

The Fox and Bensink store operated in part of the old W.J. Deuink farm implements store on West Main Street, while the Fardink barbershop operated in the other half. Seen here in 1930 are Fred Bensink (left) and Leonard Kooman (right), who ran the small service station with a gas pump out front and a single service bay workshop, with the usual soda pop bottle crates and candy bars for sale to the kids in town.

Clymer's proximity to Lake Erie and being in a traditional snowbelt has at times led to record snowfall over the years, sometimes reaching over 200 inches a year. The snowplow crew of Larry Rhebergen (left) and Harold Bensink (right) worked hard to create a single lane of traffic through a four-foot snowdrift, seen here in 1965.

The Mohawk Milk Plant crew gathered here in 1911 under the huge water supply tower for the plant. With employee numbers approaching 50 individuals, the plant was the major employer during its years of operation in the first half of the 20th century.

Many farmers in the Clymer area who had maple tree woodland took advantage of an additional opportunity to create income in the late winter by making maple syrup. With downtime created by not being able to tend to the farm fields, farm families went to work in the woods. In the photograph at right, Bert Lictus is tapping trees on his sugarbush south of town close to the state line with Pennsylvania. Spiles were tapped into the tree, and buckets hung to gather sap. When the buckets were full, they were gathered in tanks, like that in the photograph below, and returned to the sugarhouse, where the boiling process began reducing 40 gallons of sap into one gallon of syrup. (Below, courtesy of Madalene Edwards.)

Caflisch Lumber Company at one time had major operations located on Jaquin's Pond. Taking advantage of the water supply, in part created by the Tenpas hydroelectric dam downstream, allowed the company to move logs and lumber more easily, and as seen in this photograph and the next two, a water flume connects both banks of the pond. The photograph above shows logs being lifted from a holding pond to the cutting saw.

From the cutting saw, the rough-cut lumber was sent across the pond (above) to the railroad siding (below).

During what is referred to as the "Blizzard of 1936," the center of town was mired in piles of snow, making driving around town very difficult. By this time, the Eagle Hotel had been torn down and replaced with a gas station. Also barely visible is the town's water tower, having been moved from the Tenpas building just a few years earlier.

When the brick high school was built in 1913, the White school was moved across the street and, at the time of this photograph in the 1940s, served as the Grange League Federation (GLF) cooperative egg distributor station. In later years, the building was used by Meyerink Milling Company as a warehouse. Its demise came from the weight of heavy snowfall in 2002 when it collapsed.

J.W. Newhouse operated a wagon and harness shop on the south side of East Main Street in the building now occupied by the Dutch Village Restaurant. Seen here in 1905, the store was very busy, even after the arrival of the automobile. The neighboring Flickinger grocery, which became today's post office, had not yet been built.

The Henry Wassink farm located at the southern end of the pond along Mill Street was a good example of dozens of dairy farms located around Clymer. With well-maintained buildings and fine-looking herds of primarily Holstein cattle, the dairy industry remained a major part of the economy throughout the 20th century.

During the Blizzard of 1936, Clymer received more than its share of snowfall, which made it difficult to keep the streets plowed and clear. The accumulation is evident in this photograph taken in front of today's fire hall looking eastward on Main Street. Notable are the porticos on both the Cordia Garage and the Stanton Building as well as the gasoline pump at the Cordia Garage.

When the Hinckley house was torn down in the late 1930s from neglect and disrepair, in large part due to the Great Depression, it was replaced by the Texaco gas station shown in this photograph. It also was used as an automobile undercoat shop operated by Bob Bailey and a service shop by Gallup and TenHaken. It was finally torn down in the early 1980s.

The Mohawk Milk plant was a busy place as area farmers brought their milk cans to be processed daily. As can be seen in this photograph from 1912, a couple of farmers and their horse-drawn wagons deliver dozens of cans of fresh milk to be condensed and shipped off to market.

Although the milder shores of Lake Erie were 30 miles away, some Clymer residents ventured to Ripley and Westfield for seasonal work as grape pickers, as seen in this photograph from 1911. From left to right are (first row) Sophronia Eames, Jennie Spetz, Harris Mead, Jennie (Duink) Beckerink, and Eunice (Schruers) Lyons; (second row) Fred Newhouse, Lester LaCroix, Valerie Mead, W.W. Mead, and Gerald Mead.

When spring arrived, the plowing and fitting of fields took place in preparation for planting crops for the growing season. The grain crops planted most frequently were corn and oats, while alfalfa and other grasses were for hay. In this photograph, Lawrence Beckerink guides his two-horse team as he plants corn on his farm on Brownell Road in the 1930s.

In the years following World War II, the tractor made life much easier for the farmer. Although the tractor created more work, it could be done more efficiently, and summertime projects like baling hay went by quickly compared to the horse-dominant years. In this photograph from the early 1950s, Edward Oonk drives his John Deere tractor baling hay on the southwest side of town (Courtesy of Harvey Oonk.)

In 1915, John Wiggers Sr. established a business in North Clymer selling Chrysler Plymouth automobiles along with running a small grocery store and gas station. Since then, John Wiggers & Son has expanded greatly by also selling farm machinery and becoming a major dealer in maple syrup equipment. Seen here in 1930 are, from left to right, Don Hemink, Paul Wiggers, John Wiggers Sr., Charlie Seeley, and Cliff Smith. (Courtesy of the Wiggers family.)

By the 1980s, the milk plant had shut down and in 1988 was bought by the Clymer Bag Company, which used it as a warehouse and storage yard for pallet recycling. Although the trains had stopped running in the 1970s and the railroad tracks were ripped out, there was still much activity taking place, as can be seen in this aerial photograph from 1985.

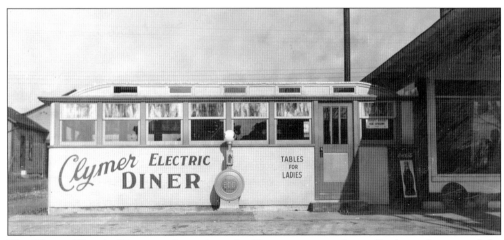

The Clymer Electric Diner was located on the Tenpas property immediately to the west of the Tenpas building. Shown here in 1931 and boasting a modern all-electric operation with "tables for ladies," an explosion in 1936 destroyed the diner and blew out windows across the street. No one was injured, and the diner was later rebuilt.

The process of creating condensed milk required a massive boiler producing enough heat to reduce the milk volume. In this photograph, Roy Crist tends to the furnace by shoveling coal and removing ash, each of which was measured for wheelbarrow weight for the accounting department.

The Kniphuisen and Croscutt hardware store occupied a newly built two-story structure at the four corners in Clymer in the late 1800s. In the photograph are, from left to right, unidentified, John Hoitink, Albert Wassink, Albert Arnink, and Florence Arnink.

Seen here in 1925 is a Ford Roadster with its axles cut narrower to accommodate wintertime bobsled tracks. The vehicle was used year-round by the electric company to read electric meters. In the photograph are, from left to right, Ray Renskers, Henry Bennink, and Garret Tenpas.

The muddy perils of a horse and buggy ride in poor weather and on unpaved roads in the early 1900s can be seen in this photograph from 1913. Taken at the four corners intersection of Clymer and in front of the Eagle Hotel, Lula Swanson and her unidentified driver were not deterred by the ankle-deep muddy condition of the roads.

Operated by James Croscutt, the corner hardware store shown here in 1923 still had many hand tools and home necessities like a butter churn and reel lawn mower. Yet it is also a Goodyear service station and sold tire chains, as seen in the window. It was Croscutt who later tore down the Hinckley house in the 1930s and built a Texaco gas station in its place on the opposite corner.

Spitzer Funeral Home and Hutton Furniture Store with Audrey's Attic operated side by side from the 1960s to the 1980s. While still called the Spitzer Funeral Home, it is now owned by David Dengler. The furniture side of the building has experienced a variety of businesses, from a flower shop and beauty shop to a credit union. Today, it is a gift shop.

Clymer has had its share of automobile dealerships over the years. Ford sales existed on West Main Street when Charles Reed began sales in 1952, expanded with the acquisition by Julian Buesink in 1960, and grew again with purchase by Gene Buesink in 1965. Although operations ended in the 1980s, business continues today as Lictus Keystone and the new Clymer Hardware.

Concrete sidewalks and curbs allowed residents easier access to the stores at the center of town and gave everyone the impression of progress being made in the early 20th century. Photographed here in 1909 are, from left to right, Jack Paul, Albert Querreveld, and James Croscutt at work laying forms on North Center Street across from the town hall.

The land around Clymer is blessed with gravel deposits left from the last Ice Age. As a result, the gravel pits provide a necessary resource in the construction of roads and buildings. Photographed here in the early 1900s are, from left to right, Will Wassink, Raymond Wassink, Dave Bensink, Garrett Wassink, Byron Wassink, Lou TeWinkle, Henry Bensink, and Bill Rhebergen loading and hauling wagons with gravel to be taken to a local worksite.

Those gravel pits provided the resources needed to lay the first concrete road leading out of Clymer to the east of town. The crew is working here in 1919 on the road to Panama and Jamestown. As the automobile became more ubiquitous, good roads became essential for travel and commerce.

The story of the emergence of Gallup and TenHaken is like other businesses in Clymer as one partner buys out another and then a marriage brings another partner into the business. Originally located at the southeast corner of the center of town, the John Deere dealership purchased the former Clymer Lumber Company, renovated it, and moved there in 1970. While the Tenpas building was being torn down, the brick building on the left also served for a short time as the bank until the new one was finished on its current site.

Whether for sport or for food, hunting wild game in the area has always been a part of life for many people living in Clymer. In the 1820s, the town offered a $5 bounty for every wolf hide turned into the town council. In this photograph from the 1940s, Howard Legters and his Uncle Packy Legters stand in front of the meat market on Main Street with three deer taken from a day's worth of hunting.

The Agway store and lumberyard located across Mill Street from the milk plant met a variety of needs of local farmers and townsfolk. Built in 1936 as a GLF (Grange League Federation) store, it had its own railroad siding for its grain, fertilizer, and lime deliveries. Farmers and gardeners alike could find all their needs, including household appliances, at Agway. As the sign says, "Supplies for home, farm, garden."

Milk bottle collectors might have a bottle or two from the TeCroney Dairy, which operated from this location on North Center Street at the edge of town. Home delivery of bottled fresh milk was available in Clymer from 1919 until 1957. As glass bottles fell out of use, TeCroney Farm continued to deliver milk cartons to schools and stores until the 1980s.

As a young teenager, Norman TeCroney stands in front of his family home on North Center Street holding the reins of his horse. TeCroney eventually established a successful milk-bottling dairy farm bearing the family name along with his sons Norvel and Nelson. Today, the TeCroney Apartments are located where the dairy barn used to stand.

Ready to make the short trip down the street to the milk plant is Henry Wassink, who has the back end of his vehicle loaded with cans from that day's milking. Just a few years earlier, Wassink was making that trip by horse and wagon.

Lictus Keystone operated from a building that at one time was the livery stable for the Eagle Hotel. Aside from being a gas station, Lictus Keystone's owner Jim Lictus also sold bicycles, motorbikes, and Arctic Cat snowmobiles. Today, this building houses an insurance agency and credit union. In the photograph below, Lictus Keystone also provided fuel deliveries to local farmers from its bulk station on Mill Street. Home delivery of heating fuel for homes as well as gasoline and diesel for farm tractors was vitally important for running the farm.

Roadbuilding around Clymer was always a sign of progress, even if much of the work was labor-intensive with shovels and horse-drawn wagons. In this photograph from 1911, workers do have the help of a steam shovel to move hillsides of dirt to create a less winding and more level roadbed. With better roads, farmers and businesses gained greater access to markets.

Located just south of the center of town was Meyerink Milling Company. As a grain feed mill business, it served local farmers by taking their harvested grain crops like corn and oats, grinding them up into formulated mixtures, and then bagging up the blend to be delivered to the dairy farmers as a supplemental feed for the dairy herd. Photographed here in 1950 are, from left to right, owner Roy Gravink, and employees Rue Button, Harry Koerselman, Ernie TeWinkle, and Harold Bensink.

Three

COMMUNITY LIFE

CHURCHES, SCHOOLS, AND CIVIC ORGANIZATIONS

While it is easy to think of everyday life in a small town as going about one's everyday work on the family farm or family business, a community is created when its people also share civic responsibilities, educate the children, and come to worship together if they so choose. Throughout its existence, the citizens of Clymer have taken pride in the academic and athletic achievement of its schools, created ways to meet individual civic obligations and responsibilities, and established churches to meet their spiritual needs. Schools always seem to unite communities because of the shared interest everyone has in a successful outcome, whether it be the graduation of the senior class or victory on the ball court. School pride is never more apparent than the time rival schools compete against each other in a championship game and much of the community turns out to cheer on their hometown team. Volunteerism also seems to be an essential element of a vibrant community, and there have been many examples of that over the years. The volunteer firemen who leave their jobs at a moment's notice to answer the fire siren do so because it is a community service needed by all. Everyone is in the same boat, and neighbors need to help neighbors when a fire breaks out or someone needs to be transported to a hospital. Other organizations like 4-H, Boy Scouts, Girl Scouts, and a variety of clubs like the Conservation Club also perform vital community service by promoting awareness of the group's cause. The churches of Clymer also serve the people in ways not always apparent. For the first Dutch immigrants, the church provided a foundation for newly arrived families to plant roots and worship in the mother tongue. Moving into the 20th century, churches not only met the needs of their congregation at the time of a baptism, wedding, or funeral, but a small number of individuals also went into the ministry or pursued missionary work. Regardless of the cause or commitment, the people of Clymer have always found a way to contribute to their community.

This was Clymer High School from 1913 to 1936. It replaced the White school, which was moved across the street and repurposed, among other businesses, as an egg distributorship This new school brought all grade levels together under one roof. Yet it did not have a gymnasium, which is why basketball games were played at the town hall. When Clymer became the first school district in Chautauqua County to centralize in 1936, this structure was disassembled, and wherever possible, materials were used in the construction of the new school and gymnasium, which survives as the oldest part of the current school.

Although many people think that competitive sports for girls began in the 1970s, in some locales, history tells a different story. This image shows the Clymer High School girls' basketball team from 1926 to 1927. The members are, from left to right, (first row) Arlene Christ, Hazel Oonk, Myrtle Croscutt, and Irene Ton; (second row) Irma Legters, Elizabeth VanderSchaaff, Marjorie Evans, Mildred Fardink, and Blanche TeWinkle.

That same 1926–1927 school year produced the following boys' basketball team. From left to right are (first row) Rake Wassink, Bernie Damcott, Marion Gallup, and John Legters; (second row) Prof. Dana King, Howard Legters, Burtis VanderSchaaff, Carlyle Neckers, Red Crist, and Byron Wassink (manager).

Abbe Reformed Church, seen here in 1910, began in 1869 as the congregation outgrew the Clymer Hill Reformed Church. As a second church for the growing Dutch population, the church membership continued to grow, reaching over 400, with another 250 affiliated with Abbe in 1950. The Abbe Reformed Church was named in 1877 for a benefactor from Albany, New York, whose gift allowed the church consistory to erase its debt.

The local 4-H Club "Eager Beavers" has long instilled the organization's motto, "Head, Heart, Hands, and Health" in young people in the Clymer area. By providing several programs from raising animals, promoting healthy living, and encouraging civic engagement, young people were better prepared for today's world. Shown here in 1980 are, from left to right, Sheila Schenk, Tim Oonk, and Milinda King. (Courtesy of Alberta and Harvey Oonk.)

In 1936, the newly opened Clymer Central School dedication took place on the front lawn and sidewalks of the school. The Damcott-Jones American Legion color guard, followed by the marching band, led the festivities. Something interesting about this particular photograph is the telephone pole with "restrooms" painted on it vertically. Prior to the school's construction, Ed TeCulver owned a gas station located at this site that was moved westward to the corner of Freeman Street, where it remains to this day.

The Clymer Hill Reformed Church, established in 1853, is seen as the "Mother Church" of Dutch settlers who began arriving in the middle of the 1800s. Located in the northern part of the town, it can easily be seen high on Ravlin Hill overlooking the town and valley to the south. As a reminder of its Dutch heritage, sermons were conducted in the Dutch language until 1917.

The Boy Scouts have long been active in the Clymer area, establishing Camp Beaver in the early 1950s close to the Clymer Conservation Club and participating in national jamborees. In this photograph from 1941 are, from left to right, (first row) Clayton Duink, Earl Duink, John Wassink, Russell Damcott, George Christensen, and Gordon Holthouse; (second row) John Bridges, Thomas Bridges, Alfred Lamparelli, Bob Wassink, Lamont Goring, Wade Quarrould, Gilbert TeWinkle, and John Neckers; (third row) Albert Kearns, Marion Alday, Ken Kooman, Clarence Rhebergen, Carlyle Neckers, Walter Coburn, and Blaine Wallace.

As a service organization, the Independent Order of Odd Fellows promotes goodwill and harmony as well as improving the character of people from all walks of life. Photographed here in the late 1940s are, from left to right, (first row) Harold Bull, Albert Arnink, Claud Lictus, and Milt Rundell; (second row) Garrett Querreveld, Preston Smith, Clifford Smith, Loren Upperman, and Floyd Arnink.

The sister organization of the Odd Fellows was the Rebekah Lodge, which served the community with the goal of friendship, love, and truth as well as providing kindness and hospitality to strangers. Included here are, from left to right, (first row) Sarah Schreurs, Eva Bull, Vera Lictus, Florence Arnink, and Clara Bensink; (second row) Hazel Smith, Mary Gabriel, Mildred Arnink, and Nellie Querreveld.

The Clymer Fire Company, created in 1921, purchased its first chemical truck in 1923. For almost two years, it was stored in Chris Christensen's car dealership until a two-bay fire hall was completed in 1924 on the site of today's fire hall. In the years since, volunteers have responded to fires and emergencies throughout the community and new vehicles and equipment have been purchased, and in 1958, a new dual-use fire hall and community building was erected.

The Clymer Conservation Club was organized in 1942, and during the summer and fall of 1948, the club constructed this Canadian balsam log clubhouse located between Clymer and North Clymer. In the summer of 1949, it hosted an all-day community picnic, including baseball games, horse-pulling contests, and fireworks. Throughout the years, the clubhouse has welcomed family reunions and wedding receptions and continues to hold archery contests and the like today.

The Clymer Fire Department recently celebrated its centennial in 2021 as it continued to meet the needs of the community. In the late 1970s, the dozens of men and women in this photograph fought fires and went out for medical emergencies as soon as they received the emergency call or heard the World War II siren blaring from the fire hall rooftop.

Townline School No. 14 is another example of the one-room school that brought neighborhood students together for a basic education of the three R's. Seen here in 1915, boys and girls are outdoors playing games, including baseball. Following the eighth grade, students who continued with their education had to travel to the high school in Clymer. Others sought out work, with many on their family farms. (Courtesy of Barbara Gayne.)

The 1950–1951 boys' basketball team brought home the first Section VI title for Clymer at a time when there was no state tournament. From left to right are (first row) Coach Eidens, Vincent Bensink, Homer Loomis Jr., Milton Courtright, Norman Cady, and Richard TenHaken; (second row) John White, Rue Button, and Harold VanEarden.

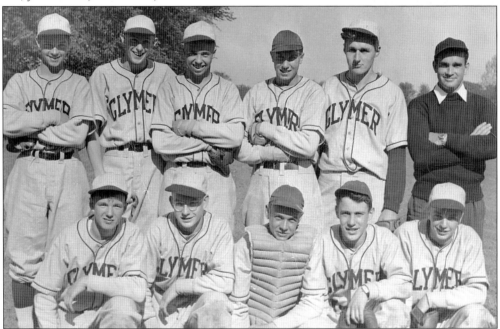

Baseball and softball are often referred to as America's pastime. The 1946 edition of the Clymer school team included, from left to right, (first row) Gordon White, Slaney Walford, Llewellyn Legters, Kenny Wilkinson, and Tab Weeks; (second row) Malcolm Boozel, Russ Bemis, Herky Porter, Robert Perdue, Paul TenHuisen, and coach Walt Colburn. Many guys like these continued to play in the summer community softball leagues with teams sponsored by local businesses, giving adult men a chance to continue their favorite pastime that began on the high school baseball diamond.

Shown here in 1929, the "Little Red School House," as it is affectionately referred to today, served as District School No. 5 and functioned as such until centralization in the late 1930s. Registered as a National Historic Landmark, it survives today and is maintained as a working museum, hosting for two days a year, elementary students who get to experience a one-room schoolhouse education from 100 years ago, including drawing water from an outdoor pump.

The Abbe Reformed Church Consistory is the governing body of elders and deacons of the church and, with the leadership of the reverend, is elected to carry out the spiritual and financial needs of the church. Seen here in 1919 are, from left to right, (first row) Henry VanEarden, John Wassink, J.W. Legters, Henry Legters, and Albert Oonk; (second row) Henry Gravink, Albert Neckers Jr., Rev. John Bennink, Garret Tenpas, William Dunnewold, and Henry Schreurs.

TEACHER'S CONTRACT

I _Florence TeWinkle_ of _Clymer_

county of _Chaut_ a duly qualified teacher, hereby contract

with the board of { education / ~~trustees~~ } of district no. _3_ town of _Clymer_ county of

Chaut to teach _3 & 4 Grades_ in

Clymer High School of the said district for the term of

also to take turns with other teachers to remain during noon hours to maintain order

_40_ consecutive weeks, except as hereafter provided, commencing _Sept_ 19_29_

at a ~~yearly~~ compensation of $_1150 oo_ payable in _10_ installments, at the end of

each _Month_ during the term of such employment.

And the board of { education / ~~trustees~~ } of said district hereby contracts to employ said teacher, for said

period, at said rate of compensation, payable at the times herein stated.

Said board of { education / ~~trustees~~ } reserve the right to provide for a vacation or vacations of not more

than _4_ weeks in the aggregate, which vacation shall not count as a part of the term of service

above referred to.

Four per cent of the amount of each order or warrant issued in payment of the compensation required to be paid hereunder shall be deducted as provided by the Education Law relative to the State Teachers Retirement Fund.

Dated _Mar 19_ 19_29_

Florence TeWinkle Teacher

W. L. Schreurs } Board of Education or Trustees

This Contract to be Void if not signed and returned on or before Mar 29

This contract shall be executed in duplicate and one copy thereof given to the teacher and one retained by the board.

Teachers for the one-room schoolhouses received the necessary preparation and certification from the state and were hired to teach where needed. Some taught at the one-room, multigrade district schools scattered around the township, while others taught in town at the multiroom schoolhouse. This is an example from 1929 of the yearly contracts signed by teachers; in this case, Florence (TeWinkle) Legters. It increased to $75 a year for three years until she married Howard Legters and, by contractual restrictions, had to stop teaching. (Courtesy of Loujean White.)

Sunday school classes provided religious lessons for members of the church that went beyond the Sunday morning sermon. In the photograph above are Sam Ton's 1915 high school girls' class members; from left to right are (first row) Iva Neckers, Velma (Neckers) Elliott, Marion (Kruiselbrink) Meyerink, Elsie (Hewes) Legters, and Laura (Neckers) Caflisch; (second row) Ethel (Claney) Schurman, Esther Ton, Dena (Habink) Hogenboom, Ruth (Tenpas) Gravink, Coral (Legters) Groters, and Carol (Neckers) Compton; (third row) Sam Ton, Christina (Simmelink) Renskers, Maybelle (Ton) Gravink. Below is Albert Neckers Jr.'s 1915 high school boys' class, including, from left to right, (first row) Henry Rhebergen, Ruben Schruise, Walter TeWinkle, Fred Dunnewold, James Wassink, and Jay Gravink; (second row) Albert Neckers Jr., Ben Schruise, Orin Schurman, Clarence Rhebergen, Walter Schreurs, and Delbert Neckers; (third row) Jesse Holthouse, George Legters, Lewis Holthouse, Edward Ton, Loren Bakerink, Leslie Fardink, and Frank Vanderkooi.

A Vacation Bible School (VBS) class is assembled here in 1948 in front of the Abbe Reformed Church. The school offered kids of all ages from around town a chance for religious education, fun, and games while school was out of session for the summertime.

Cornelius Tenpas, son of Garret Tenpas, headed off to Hope College in Holland, Michigan, in the fall of 1926. It was a long drive of about 150 miles, and his education prepared him for life as a missionary overseas. Unfortunately, an untimely death at home during the summer of 1928 ended that goal.

The first church in Clymer was the Baptist Church, established in 1829. Although it likely was not the first structure erected, the building seen here located on Freeman Street served as the Baptist church from 1841 until 1868 when the brick church, later known as the Tenpas building, was constructed on East Main Street. The Baptist congregation disbanded in the late 1800s.

The White school served as the schoolhouse for the children of the village of Clymer from 1880 until 1913. In this photograph from 1911, the school's setting is approximately the same as the current school. When the first brick school was built in 1913; this structure was moved across the street and, in later years, served as an egg distributorship and warehouse for Meyerink Milling Company until its collapse from heavy snow in 2001.

A very practical high school education for an agricultural community like Clymer included a hands-on lesson given by Prof. William Frisbee with a horse, as seen in the photograph above from 1920. During the mid-20th century, the school's Future Farmers of America (FFA) organization, as seen below in 1956, provided students with classes designed to educate successful farmers and leaders in the agricultural community. Local and statewide competitions gave members an opportunity to show off their skills in cattle judging and machinery operation.

By 1939, the Clymer Fire Department had constructed a two-bay fire hall and purchased a Dodge fire truck, and both are seen here at the current location of today's fire hall. In the photograph are, from left to right, Blaine Wallace, Harold Bull, Art Howles, Harold Legters, Clarence Rhebergen, Ken Kooman, and Homer Loomis Sr.

The Clymer graduating class of 1924 included, from left to right, (first row) Mildred Bensink, Fred Dunnewold, and Florence (TeWinkle) Legters; (second row) Henrietta Kots, W. Whitney, Florence Legters, Arthur Goggin, and Mabel (Damcott) TenHuisen.

The Clymer Methodist Church began in 1825. Located close to the center of town, its tall steeple rising above the trees could easily be seen from the surrounding hills and countryside. Interestingly, the Methodist and Baptist churches shared a bell in the late 1800s. With services held at different times and with the bell hanging in the Baptist church, the Methodist sexton had to walk over to the Baptist church to ring the bell for the Methodist worship service. When the Baptist congregation disbanded, the bell was moved to the Methodist church.

At the time of this photograph in 1916, the Stanton Building served as the post office, telephone office, and theater. Aside from the performers posing for the camera on the sidewalk out front on the sidewalk, a sign on the corner of the building promoted the Tuesday evening motion pictures being shown in the theater on the second floor.

This ornately adorned home with an inviting front porch was built in 1825 and still stands today on the corner of Maple Avenue where the Countertop Solutions showroom is located. Serving as Clymer School No. 3, it was paid for in wheat and students were required to supply a quarter cord of wood two feet in length as tuition. When the White school was built after 1881, this school became a home, as seen here in the late 1800s. Notice the two front entrance doors for boys and girls.

When the school district was centralized in 1936, it included Clymer, French Creek, and a narrow sliver of Harmony townships. This explains the lettering on this school bus in 1937, which was maroon, unlike the traditional yellow school buses.

Four

CELEBRATING LIFE
FESTIVALS, PARADES,
AND ACCOMPLISHMENTS

Clymer remains the type of community that takes great pride in its heritage and individual achievements. As the saying goes, everyone loves a parade, and throughout the years, Clymer has had their share, from the celebration of Independence Day to the festivities associated with the Tulip Festival. The tradition of parades existed before World War I, especially with the Fourth of July celebration, and until the advent of the Tulip Festival in the mid-1950s, the mid-summer parade and town picnic in Damcott's Grove south of town was the celebration of the year. When, in 1953, the Community Club proposed a springtime Saturday to clean the streets and sidewalks of Clymer in a *schoonmaken tag*, translated loosely as "make clean day," little could they have imagined how successful that idea would become over the years as the Tulip Festival and the celebration of Clymer's Dutch heritage. Today, that heritage is on full display, not just during the Tulip Festival, but year-round for all to see as four red windmills welcome the traveler to Clymer from all directions leading into town as many come to visit the Dutch Village Restaurant.

While the Tulip Festival celebrates the collective heritage of the town, a number of individuals have provided leadership and foresight to the Clymer community. Some have given of themselves in public service as elected officials, others in military service, and still others as business leaders. Individuals like Albert Neckers Jr., Ralph Thompson, Garret Tenpas, and many others over the years have led Clymer's development and progress. Regardless of their contribution or achievement, they collectively add to the heritage of Clymer.

In the 1920s and 1930s, the young men of Clymer came together essentially as a semiprofessional basketball team. Competing against neighboring communities prior to high school contests, the Flying Dutchmen played its games on the second floor of the town hall. Pictured for the 1930–1931 season are, from left to right, (first row) Harold Legters, Red Crist, Cutch Legters, and Marion Gallup; (second row) Phil Skeps, Carlyle Neckers, John Legters, Rake Wassink, Byron Wassink, and Norm Neckers.

The arrival of springtime meant the Tulip Festival was just around the corner. This also meant that people would dig out their authentic Dutch costumes and wooden shoes, school kids would practice traditional klompen (wooden shoe) dancing, and preparations would be made for that day in May when tulips were in full bloom, the streets were scrubbed, a parade took place, and a Tulip Queen was crowned. Seen here in 1955 is the Thompson family all dressed up for a full day's worth of activities.

The Tulip Festival gave every business in town the chance to spruce up for spring by washing the windows and cleaning the sidewalks of their winter grime. In this photograph, Meyerink Milling Company has planted a tulip bed and painted a sign advertising its belief it provided some of the best cattle feed in the area.

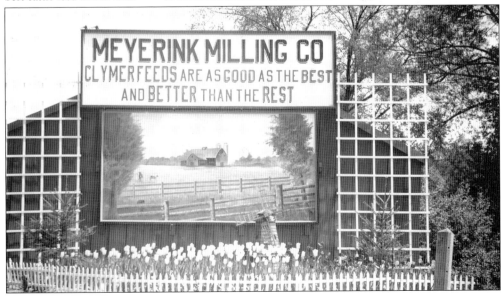

Clymer's citizens were always prepared to defend their country when called upon to serve. As seen in this 1918 advertisement from W.J. Deuink machinery sales, those area men and women were listed on this World War I honor roll. Most of these men returned to Clymer and became charter members of the Damcott-Jones American Legion, which met for some time in the Stanton Building.

After the Memorial Day parade in 1919, Clymer's World War I veterans marched as a unit and posed for photographs, here with Civil War veterans. Seated in front are, from left to right, Clyde Howles and Clarence Spitzer; (second row) Blaine Wallace, Civil War veterans A.W. Thompson and W.J. Dunnewold, and Wilmer Hodges; (third row) Jesse Holthouse, Clarence Legters, Clarence Vruink, Clifford Legters, Jay Tenpas, Roy Gravink, Gilbert Ton, Clarence Rhebergen, and Walter Schruers.

The Tulip Festival parade celebrated Clymer's Dutch heritage in many ways. Although many people could claim Dutch ancestry, everyone in town found a way to participate. Many boys and girls from school learned traditional klompen (wooden shoe) dancing for performing during the parade, as seen here in 1955.

The Clymer Central School marching band participated in the 1955 Tulip Parade, and as the years went by, bands from many neighboring schools and organizations also made the trip to Clymer to contribute to the musical festivities of the day.

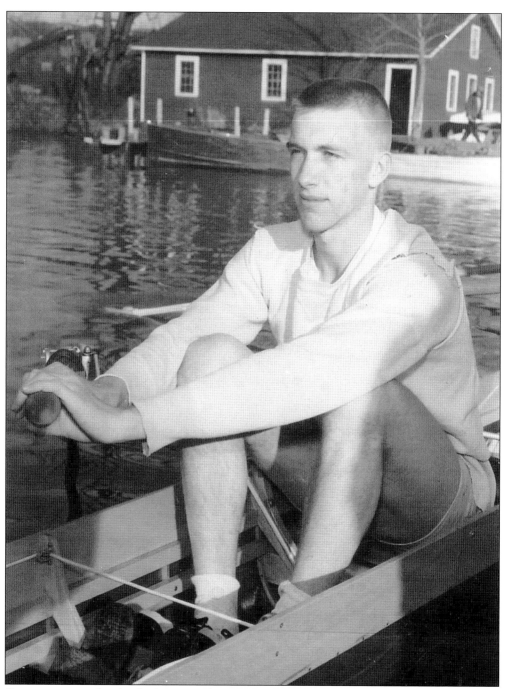

Growing up on the family farm in Clymer, Philip Gravink (1935–2020) reached heights in the rowing and skiing world few have achieved. He crewed Cornell to four national collegiate championships as well as a gold medal performance at the Royal Henley Regatta in 1957. Returning to Clymer, he cofounded Peek-n-Peak Ski area in 1963, was honored as a 2012 inductee to the National Ski and Snowboard Hall of Fame, and served in various advisory capacities in the skiing industry, especially in New England. (Courtesy of the Chautauqua Sports Hall of Fame.)

Unique to Clymer to this day, annual May Day celebrations began in 1939 with festivities on the front lawn of the high school and included young girls winding a Maypole, class representatives carrying lilac-laden arches, and a queen holding court. Here, in 1955, the queen is Charlene Damon. This was also the first year a Tulip Queen was crowned.

This Neckers Company float has all the flags and patriotic bunting associated with a Fourth of July celebration. The float served as an advertisement for the dry goods business with brand names such as Kellogg's, Post, and the National Biscuit Company along with everyday clothing items.

These two aerial photographs of Clymer were taken in 1962. The photograph above shows a view looking westward toward the center of town, in which the school, tennis courts, and Methodist church are clearly visible. The view at left faces south down Mohawk Street, with the school and pond in sight. There is also a small dirt track by the pond.

At the 1956 Tulip Festival, Burgermeister Harold Legters honored Netherlands-born residents living in Clymer. Seen here are, from left to right, Burgermeister Legters and residents James Cordia, John Volk, Albert Bensink, and Henry Lemeness, with Garret Tenpas standing in back.

Photographed in front of the Tenpas building in May 1919, recently returned World War I soldiers stand in formation during the Memorial Day parade. These veterans formed the Damcott-Jones American Legion Post in memory of John Damcott and Walter Jones, who lost their lives in the Argonne Forest of France in 1918.

Lt. Dale Spencer (1922–2016), a 1940 Clymer graduate, shot down four enemy aircraft in less than one minute on a single mission over Germany on May 29, 1944. Awarded the Distinguished Service Cross and Distinguished Flying Cross with three oak leaf clusters, Lieutenant Spencer went on to become a double ace by the war's end and thrilled the residents of Clymer in 1945 as he flew his P-51 low over the town, dipping his wing tips in salute to the town that raised him. Spencer moved to and then retired in Southern California, and the Navy's Blue Angels paid tribute to him at the Los Angeles County Air Show upon his death in 2016.

A humorous Legters Brothers float from the 1958 Tulip Festival depicts the "weenie raft" at work, processing hot dogs. In an assembly line manner, an unsuspecting dog disappears into a meat grinder and a sausage comes out the other end, to the dismay of all the children in the parade crowd witnessing such a sleight of hand.

This float from post–World War I honors Clymer's contribution to the war effort. The small stars on the banner at the front of the float signify the number of soldiers from Clymer and the three large stars note three lives lost fighting in France, those being John Damcott, Walter Jones, and Merle Raspas. A fourth, Roy Willink, died in Texas training as a pilot.

At the 1954 Tulip Festival, town residents signed a letter to Queen Juliana of the Netherlands commemorating the 1944 Allied liberation of the Dutch city of Nijmegen. Signing at the table are John Volk and Gertrude Volk Legters. Looking on are, from left to right, Garret Tenpas, Garret Boland, James Cordia, Henry Lemeness, Henry Querreveld, and Albert Bensink.

On the day of the Tulip Parade, the burgermeister examines the dirty streets and pronounces the need for scrubbing them clean. In this photograph from 1954, women are at work with pails of water and brushes cleaning the sidewalk in front of the school on East Main Street. Scattered down Main Street were watering troughs used by men with yoke and buckets to dump water on the streets with women and children following to give the thoroughfare a good cleaning.

Dr. Lorenzo P. McCray (1851–1924) arrived in Clymer in 1880 and saw to the medical needs of Clymer citizens for 45 years. Becoming a highly respected community servant, he served as town supervisor from 1896 to 1921 as well as director of the Clymer State Bank.

Always eager to turn out for a parade, townsfolk, young and old, gather in front of the Eagle Hotel to celebrate the Fourth of July in 1925. At that time, the hotel was owned by Elmer Croscutt, James Croscutt, and Chris Christensen and was in its last years of existence. By the 1930s, having outlived its usefulness, it disappeared from the town's landscape.

The culmination of every Tulip Festival is the crowning of the Tulip Queen. Crowned in 1956 was Loujean (Legters) White, seated here surrounded by her court and young attendants. The candidates in the back row included, from left to right, Nancy Mathews, Joyce Wilde, Joanne TenHaken, Judy Camp, and Marlene Redding. Attendant children were, from left to right, Ted Mathews, Debbie Williams, Judy McCray, and Curt Wiggers.

One of the traditions of the Tulip Festival was the baby buggy parade, seen here in 1961. Families often passed a buggy down from generation to generation as a family heirloom, and the Tulip Parade gave recently new mothers the chance to participate with their infant children.

In what could have been a scene played out across Clymer every time families and kids got together for some special occasion like a family reunion, three cousins pose for a photograph for their parents. Seen here in 1935 are, from left to right, Richard TenHaken, Charlotte (Legters) TeWinkle, and Carolyn (Wevers) Beckerink.

For many years, Amos VanEarden carried on and kept alive a family tradition that his grandfather brought from the Netherlands. Using the same hand tools and wooden bench of his grandfather, VanEarden is shown here in 1957 at the Tulip Festival making wooden shoes. The tools and workbench can be seen today at the historical society.

OPEN MEETING

C.C.S. AUDITORIUM

THURSDAY   FEB. 12
8:00 P.M.

COME AND LEARN MORE

ABOUT   THE

HOLLAND-IMPROVEMENT
PROJECT

FOR   CLYMER

SPEAKER-PROF.ORA SMITH

OF CORNELL UNIVERSITY

COLORED SLIDES of HOLLAND

FREE

ADMISSIOM AND REFRESHMENTS

SPONSORED   BY
CLYMER COMMUNITY CLUB

Everyone Invited   *Free*   *Free*   *Everyone Invited*

In February 1953, a town meeting sponsored by the Clymer Community Club was held to discuss ideas that would eventually lead to what is known today as the Tulip Festival. As seen in this image, the flier mentions the "Holland Improvement Project." Two months later during the last weekend in April, *schoonmaken tag*, or "make clean day," was held; the streets were cleaned; and the groundwork was laid for future windmills, tulip beds, and a parade to celebrate Clymer's Dutch heritage.

Part of the springtime May Day ceremony included two memorable steps during the event. As seen in the photograph above from 1942 at the west end of the school, class attendants carry arches wrapped with lilac blooms to get things started. In the photograph below from 1956, another step included elementary girls skipping through the arches and then winding the Maypole by weaving in and out and around the pole until finished. (Both, courtesy of Marlea Brown.)

Garret Tenpas, seen at right in a photograph from 1960, is an example of the American dream where an immigrant makes good. His successes as a US citizen from a small town are immense. An entrepreneur in every sense of the word, he was a businessman who played a large part in the development of Clymer during the first half of the 1900s, and throughout this book, the name Tenpas is connected to many aspects of that growth. In the image below, the advertisement describes a patented device invented by Tenpas to level the axle of a threshing machine essential to farmers.

Celebrating the Fourth of July in 1923 was an opportunity for the community to have a parade with floats, decorated cars, and marching bands. In this photograph, Josh Hogenboom drives a car for Legters Brothers. If one looks closely, the lettering on the car is made from dozens of hot dogs affixed to both sides of the car.

The Fourth of July celebration began with a parade through town and proceeded to Damcott Grove south of town for a community ox roast and picnic. During the afternoon, festivities included numerous games and activities such as tug of war, pancake baking, and, as seen here in 1948, a baby contest. In the evening, a fireworks display brought a conclusion to the day's events.

This photograph of the YWCA float from the Fourth of July parade in 1920 was taken in front of the Flickinger store on East Main Street. The view on the street is one of decorated storefronts wrapped in bunting with American flags flying all over town for the Independence Day celebration.

In 1953, costumed marchers take to the streets in the first parade that soon became known as the Tulip Festival. During this initial year of springtime community festivities, these dancers performed an operetta titled *Tulip Time*, directed by Lucille Rorabeck.

The agricultural nature of Clymer is revealed in this photograph of a festooned "Clymer Farmers Feed the World" automobile float from 1919. Exactly how much is hard to determine, but in the years following World War I, Clymer's farmers greatly increased their production beyond what was consumed locally.

The annual planting of tulip beds and construction of windmills around Clymer began in 1953 as part of the Clymer beautification project. Within just a few years, the tulip beds and red windmills became a focal point of attraction for the Tulip Festival itself. As can be seen in these two photographs, crowds came to admire the floral displays at Buesink Ford on the west side of town (above) and across from the school on the corner of Mohawk Street (below). (Below, courtesy of Marlea Brown.)

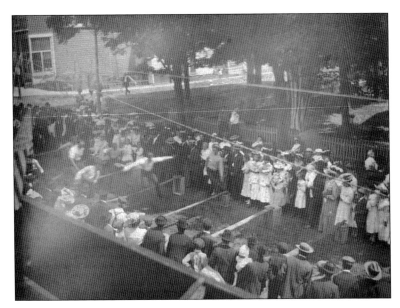

This photograph is from a late-1890s Fourth of July parade and shows some sort of foot race over makeshift hurdles taking place on West Main Street. Taken in front of the Hinckley house and the stores on the opposite side of the street, everyone appears dressed in their finest attire for such a patriotic occasion.

The Tulip Festival included the crowning of the Tulip Queen, and the Tulip Parade included a float for each queen candidate sponsored by any number of businesses and organizations. In 1950, queen candidate Nancy (Mathews) White was sponsored by the Future Farmers of America, and the float was pulled along the parade route by, from left to right, Vincent Legters, Harvey Oonk, Norvel TeCroney, Vincent Bensink, Irving Legters, and Roger Dunnewold.

Gathered on the front lawn of the school prior to the Tulip Festival parade in 1961 are youngsters from Clymer all dressed up in their authentic Dutch costumes. Some of them were participating as klompen (wooden shoe) dancers, while others helped the adults with the street scrubbing before the marching bands performed and the floats commenced down Main Street.

In an aerial photograph from 1964, the parade route of the Tulip Festival and the size of the crowd can be seen along Main Street. Buses brought neighboring school marching bands, the Shriners from Erie brought their go-karts, many businesses built their own floats, some organizations held a chicken barbecue, and numerous vendors sold cotton candy, popcorn, and all the usual festival souvenirs.

Although the Tulip Festival did not crown its first queen for another year, the 1954 May Queen, Shirley (Damon) Gravink, and her court of attendants graced the front lawn of the high school. While the Tulip Festival only occurs now in even years, the May Day celebration and crowning of a queen takes place every springtime, giving all students the experience of participation.

As was done in World War I, Clymer recognized those serving in World War II with an honor board located just to the east of the Spitzer Funeral Home. Although the number of servicemen and women from the area far exceeded World War I from 25 years prior only two lives were lost from 1942 to 1945.

A new chapter in Clymer's history began in the 1970s when members of the Amish community arrived in the area. Again, as in the past, hardworking, entrepreneurial families reinvigorated the local economy as new small businesses and a couple of large ones popped up around town. In the photograph above, a hitching post can be found where the town hall once stood, and on many country roads, a horse and buggy can frequently encounter an automobile. The Amish contribution to the future Clymer is a certainty, and the next chapter of this book is yet to be written. (Both, courtesy of Jane Babcock.)

DISCOVER THOUSANDS OF LOCAL HISTORY BOOKS FEATURING MILLIONS OF VINTAGE IMAGES

Arcadia Publishing, the leading local history publisher in the United States, is committed to making history accessible and meaningful through publishing books that celebrate and preserve the heritage of America's people and places.

Find more books like this at
www.arcadiapublishing.com

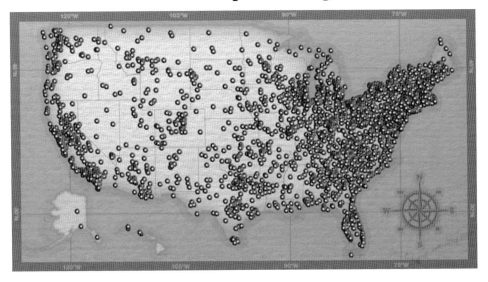

Search for your hometown history, your old stomping grounds, and even your favorite sports team.